The Eye of Tony Hicks

Poems from the Beatnik Housewife

beatnikhousewife@hotmail.com

Hollies!!
You're heroes and they're writing poetry about you.

BH

When Life Roars,
Crowd-Like
[or, The Hicks Syndrome]

Monday was rot
with the local social workers
having a conference
in the public library
so I had to re-brew the coffee
TWICE in my piddly two-hour shift
at the coffee shop.
Tuesday, aged 37, and January
I discovered a Hollies song
gone overlooked
in my teenaged obsession
with them
in the late '80's
A very cheesy love song
but brilliant
[being them
and 1968]
and I later would have been
[affectionately?] ridiculed
by my college-radio peers
for playing it
but would have
played the hell out of it
none the less.
And that single
Tuesday-37-January song
slapped me toward the grandiose
transformed me
pitched me headlong
into mad puppy-love
for the guitarist
(I had already loved him
when fourteen

but now could waste
a housewife-afternoon
gazing at YouTube performances
—a luxury I would have
faked illness for in 1988).
And that one song
led to the writing of another
and three short stories
and red-hot boudoir elation with husband
diligent guitar practice
the mending of an old mod coat lining
and better eating:
more lentils and greens
--inspired higher
healthier living as a whole
with the exception of smoking cigarettes.
Seemingly
they all did
back in those days
and it makes me feel close to them.

When we're old
I'll be like that old man at the mall
barking at his woman
'You never wanted to come along
to my VFW meetings!'

Or I'll be the senile and gape-jawed old wife
remembering only secret lies of pride
stories concocted of
beat groups
fur coats
time-travel
delicious heartbreak

'You were a bitch!' he'll whinny
'I told Brian Jones not to go in the water'
my emphysemic & demented retort.

[Oh, too-rolly-ay]

Naomi had been strongly influenced by pop culture
which she blamed indirectly
for her habit of regarding her youngest niece
as something of a scourge

It was nothing personal.

Influences included:
The Brady Bunch
The Partridge Family
Family Ties
Growing Pains
(in those days any time the show gets stale you the mother just become pregnant, that's all
Kind of like life)
Just the Ten of Us
Hanson—the pop band fraught with siblings
Little Women starring Winona Ryder
It's a Wonderful Life
and all of them had caused her to want a whole mess of children
but that didn't work out.
And the Niece in Question was born at a time when
Naomi was really striving to be pregnant
but the heavens frowned down on her
and shut her fallopian tubes with force

with the heavy sucking click-clang of a round bank-vault door

and whirled the wheel with thorough finality and a nod of satisfied task-completion.

It was for that reason she never COULD laugh appreciatively

at the little-niece stories

though the child was clearly the life of the party

like the time she put cupcake all over her face —aged four—

and announced to her mother that she'd been

re-enacting the piggy scene from A Christmas Story

[yes she used the word 're-enacting']

Oh jolly tee hee

And what a horrid aunty

Naomi

bilious head-up-ass

nigh unto slimeball

herself the scourge all along.

[Inked]

We were SOMEWHERE I had to keep the boy quiet
so I let him draw on
my palm with a blue inkpen
and that night it stained the bath tub
but I don't get stern about things of that nature.
It reminded me of my teenage years
when once
my dad inked a heart
with an arrow through it
on my sleeping mother's thigh
and it imprinted on the toilet seat
like a stamp.
It was there for ages
and being teenagers
my sister and I laughed
uproariously
giggled
insufferable
til hell wouldn't have it again.

[The Hicks-DeShannon Syndrome]

Well every day this week waiting for the school bus to bring the boy home

I smoked a cigarette on the corner and dammit I wasn't going to today

In fact I was going to pick him up early from school to prevent it

but didn't want to interfere with his 100th-day-of-kindergarten festivities

so then I *still* wasn't going to smoke that 5th cigarette of the week but I did

and here's why

It's a terrible reason:

Like a fool I squandered precious life-minutes on the internet

where someone had posted the superb

Tony Hicks Tribute #2

just photos flashing

against a marvelous Jackie DeShannon song

and Tony Hicks in his mind-wrecking mid-to-late-1960's splendor

with the fur coats and plaid jackets the audacious bangs

and bedroom eyes clear blue and smoldering

all tangled up with the painful beauty of the song,

the type of song that shouts at you "1965!" and you're *there*

in the Ben Franklin Five-and-Dime on Winner Road purchasing hair curlers

—and the bangs and the furs and I tried to play along on my guitar

So all together it was too clutching and lovely and I nearly cried

—jackass!! Don't *cry* at the long-ago beauty of an English guitarist however intense—

and desiring very much not to go through with crying

I smoked a cigarette clean down to the filter

and STILL the school bus didn't come

so I stood around wishing I were beautiful like Jackie DeShannon

and also that I could sing that way

and felt guilty about my little trail of cigarette butts

left on the corner all week long

and picked up the three I could find

and held them in my hand kept inside the pocket

of my mod plaid and fur-trimmed coat

then threw them in the kitchen trash once home.

And thinking again of Jackie DeShannon singing about heaven

and touching tongue to mouth-sore

I figured I would beat Tony Hicks to those pearly gates

because he wasn't holding a cigarette in one single Tribute #2 photo.

They were very much a vocal band and he seemed to carry himself

with an air of responsibility.

And that's ironic because

when I first stumbled on *Tony Hicks Tribute #2*

I thought it must mean that he had died.

[Hem v. Sunshine]

Reading *The Paris Wife*
about that rat Hemingway
(though I've loved him—dammit—
these eighteen years)
discovered I was the wildly jealous type
but wait a minute
knew that anyway
having married a family-counselor
whose field is 90% women I'd say.
One colleague in his classes
a woman from India
with husband & children
but would stare intensely at him and say,
"You fascinate me.
I want to know more about you"
and I wanted to fly out of my skin
and whip her toward the moon
by her braid
because we were newly married.
But then
with the same hot-curry intensity
she complimented
 the Tang Pie I'd made for the picnic:
"It is magnificent.
It is the most wonderful American flavor."

And now ten years on

I shake with admiration

for the fierce loyalty of that man

and how little worry

he ever causes me.

And that is no small favor

for one of my crippling pride

and sketchy psychological pedigree.

[Friday in February]

Today we made love at 2 o'clock in the afternoon
and he asked me to wear my black silk nightie
only I couldn't find it.
"You hung it on the bathroom doorknob" he kept saying
"Yes but that was a long time ago and I've moved it someplace mysterious now."
So I put on the pale green crepe slip I'd made before we were married
from a Folkways pattern a reprint from the 1920's.
It has little built-in shorts with a button-up crotch and
I had sewed on tiny old-fashioned tortoiseshell buttons.
I lifted the skirt to reveal the clever shorts
but he was dismayed
"That's going to be a problem"
and he meant for the logistics of lovemaking.
But I called his attention to the tiny tortoiseshell buttons
and I think he rather enjoyed unfastening them.
Usually we have an unspoken code
about bedding each other absolutely naked
but now and again we let fashion play a role
and this was one of those times.

[Quirks of Weather and Offspring]

It amazes me that our boy age six can vomit with languorous ease and no hint of panic
—he's very matter-of-fact and practical about it—
but he's completely undone and infuriated if he has to clear mucus from his throat.
Such was the case this morning,
and every time his throat needed clearing
he wanted to punch himself in the neck.
So I made him Celestial Seasonings Sugar Cookie Tea
and cooled it with tap water and added honey
and put him on my lap
and coaxed him to drink some.
He was terrified—unfamiliar hot beverage—
but once he caught the aroma
was pleased to sit there and take sips
and suddenly I wanted to do that all morning long—
cuddle and feed him tea from the red Fiestaware mug,
only I had to scurry off to my two-hour library shift
and he to school.
Now he is home for a 3-day weekend
and has a little bit of a cough
so maybe we'll get another chance at Sugar Cookie Tea.

[Growl]

When he plays the guitar
with unbridled joy
I want pettishly
nothing more than to scowl at him
because
when I turned to guitar
for solace and sense of control
three years ago

a time of
what seemed
tragic upheaval
at every turn

all he could do
when I played
was steal the joy

pick apart my
strumming style
& wax critical
of my neglecting
scale drills

and pick and pick
and pick

so that I
dreaded to go near
a guitar when
he was in the house

and hardly touched
it for a whole
year

and now that
I love it again

I wish he would
go away and
stick to the bass.

[But what of the Dear Little Hatchet-Shaped Cookie Cutter...?]

Presidents' Day
and everyone wants hot water!
Ginger Tea
Hot Chocolate
Chamomile
Green Tea
Peppermint
and behind the public-library coffee stand
I am back & forth
two hours
constantly boiling water
like a midwife.
Celebrate Presidents' Day with a hot drink!
For our part
come noon
and the boy off school
we'll keep the day
playing Lincoln Logs
and baking Dolley Madison's
Caramel-Frosted Layer Cake
and probably listening to the Zombies
because I'm in the mood for that.

[As for the hatchet cookie cutter...
Lizzie Borden day will be here before you know it...]

[Popside Darling]

It seems I had you all wrong dear Sweden
vilifying your daughters right and left in my fiction
for being leggy
blonde
and out to seduce otherwise-cherished Englishmen
When all the while we cherished
—you and I—
the same pop bands
and you very generously
let them clamber over your industrial playgrounds
and caught the whole thing on film
for the sake of art
so that I though not born yet
could breathe along
and beam and fall sideways
and feel the cold wind off the lake
and it *does* tangle up my mind some
so that
perhaps I should hate you for it
but I
never
ever
shall do.

[Blue-eyed Musiker; This One Lost]

He killed himself in 1996
just *two years* after I'd seen him last
[and bought that lovely sweet T-shirt
where IS it now
that was eighteen years ago]
Courtney Love's band played
Chicago
some time
after his death
and performed a song of his
[Valerie Loves Me]
and then she
[legs astride & guitar slung low]
raised her cigarette to the heavens
and yelled
"Give it up for that boy!"
and that had to be
the topmost tribute
to that particular dead guitarist
were *MOJO* ever to list them all…

[The ambush]

The idea of a hemorrhage
freaks me out terribly
torrents of blood
and in hearing or reading of one
I keep waiting for the afflicted to faint
until I sense a pulsing cramping of my own
and nearly faint myself
Last night nearly done reading *The Bell Jar*
came along the hemorrhage scene
and I just kept reading away like a fool
until my throat began to lurch
and ears to ring
and eyesight grow black and fuzzy around the edges
splashed water on my face
and dove for the ginger capsules under the bathroom sink
and sank to the bed
pleading feebly "Help me God…"
and tried to concentrate on innocent scenarios
involving English rock stars
recited the Lord's Prayer
and Psalm 23 put to a sad old tune
crashed into sleep
though had intended to join husband
in watching *The Twilight Zone*.
Then the problem became
how will I ever finish the book?
She's spent pages and pages engineering suicide plans

only to beg for a doctor when hemorrhaging!
What will happen next?
I must know
am dying to know
but what if the last remnants of the hemorrhage scene
should ambush my delicate sensibilities once again?
Suppose it looms up in front of my eyes while I'm driving the car
as it nearly did today
until I saved myself
turned up a pop song real loud
and let cold air in at the windows
and sang boisterously to the music?
Perhaps she wants to live now,
that girl.
Must have been the shock treatments...
Too bad they can't last forever
& she too will go in fear of the ambush.

[A little forethought for a change]

Damn.
I want to be one of those
little old ladies who smile
[unable to help it
and not from any sense of
American or matronly obligation]
at the sight of young children
clutching at their mothers
bumping into them
wailing in public when it's all too much
and naptime is overdue
smacking their little siblings
and generally being shrill...

I want to be that smiling type of old lady
all sage
and reassuring
and lightly perfumed with flowery talc
and dispensing comfort
and tales of experience
"Oh, that.
That'll work itself out.
My little Zelda was just the same."

I don't wish to be one of those
deeply-frowned old bats
still shaking her fist at God

30 or 40 years down the road
just because my little lad
will never have a brother or sister
No Zelda or Link to his Clyde
and I do find it rather mocking
[in my current state]
that those names I long favored
have emerged as characters
in a rabidly popular video game.

The deaf kid worries me
when he volunteers at the library
because he makes little moans
he can't hear himself doing
and two shelves over I worry
that he might be ill
or experiencing a bad trip
or hemorrhaging.

[Greengills Flashback]

In the crockpot there's chicken
and cumin and chili powder
and garlic powder
and the scent of it makes me greenish
in the same way goulash did
when I was first to be a mother
but I don't kid myself here.

Well I do a little

and tot up the names of
last-century musicians
after whom I would call
a welcome new puking little one

Noel-Anthony-Lincoln-Frederick
[the Frederick for the old man actually
as well as for Link Wray]
and would put Christopher in there
as it sounds so English
and so well with Anthony
only once a Christopher
betrayed my husband
by stealing his girlfriend
but that was well before.

And that's all the self-kidding I do just now

for various reasons

and God has

kindly

signaled me

that the door has closed on my childbearing

Even so

Noel Anthony Christopher Lincoln Frederick,

I'm sorry

if this cigarette

and those ginger capsules

and the gin I might enjoy later on

do you any harm

in there

hypothetically speaking

of course.

[Darling]

A very odd housewife day because at last I had four hours all to myself.

Honestly it's been a full week and a half since I've had that kind of time

and with the laundry in

really I should have been tidying the basement

or cleaning the kitchen floor

or at the very least practicing guitar

that bastard F-chord

or sketching out that fictional scene

where Esther is consoling Astrid

for being obsessed with a smug '90's Brit-Pop guitarist

but instead you know what I did?

Watched *Darling* a 1965 English film

about a model who sleeps her way to the top

and is bored with life.

Marvelous for its fashions

and instrumental music

and the song accompanying the commercial for chocolates.

Delicious horrid affairs I shall never know myself

having been drilled all through with Christian morals from an early age

and though crafted with tremendous admiration for men

also crippling shyness around all of them

save,

at first strangely,

the one I ended up marrying.

[Ode]

I love my mother-in-law
because when I decided to leave my nanny post
and marry her son
the air was thick and sour
with the strong disapproval of my parents
[not for the boy I'd chosen
rather for leaving the nanny post
before contract was up
even though I was 26
and paid the new-nanny finder's fee seriously
they are *drunk* with responsibility those two]
but my mother-in-law shared a tale
wherein she garnered the strong disapproval of her own folks
for dropping out of college after like one semester
in order to get hitched to Mark Z.
so every time I get nettled by her psychotic home-scrubbing
and bunker-style household inventory
which prepared her son
for a scatterbrain like myself *not at all*
well at such times I really must remember the above tale
and how she whipped it out at just the correct
and kind moment to soothe me
and let my heart fill up with hilarious love for her.

[Brava]

When the last plane from Texas
let us out at the St. Louis airport on New Year's Day
it was cold outside!
We'd stepped from eighty degrees into the Austin airport
and emerged into 26-degree St. Lou
and an oldish man pointedly asked our little boy, "*Where's your coat??*"
Cheery smiley I answered
"It's at Grandma's! We've been in Texas!"
but the old man wouldn't even look at me.
Soon came the in-laws to scoop us up into their minivan
and I shared the story of the old codger
with nothing better to do than judge my mothering skills
while waiting for his ride
and my mother-in-law couldn't believe her ears
and as much as called him a jackass
right there in the minivan.
And that's another reason why I love her.

[...and nowhere to go]

The housewife is a sucker
for the enticing new product
and say
that latest shampoo & conditioner
with the cheery swinging floral-patterned bottles
titillated above and beyond the call of duty!
The Mundane Everyday was
SHATTERED
by promises written right on the bottle
that my hair would ask to be touched—in French—
and possibly cause people to walk straight into street signs.
Their respective aromas turned my shins to jelly
deciding me at once
and I felt instantly 30% more gorgeous
having made the decision to buy.
I pinballed between the Vanilla-Rice-Milk-scented
[with its promises regarding street signs]
and the Cherry-Blossom-Almond-Milk
[which would teach my hair to speak French]
and favored the latter in the end
because the pinks of the bottle
would exactly match my shower curtain.
And lo & behold
one week later
while brushing my
[fragrant!]
hair in the morning

the old man happened by and
[seldom given to such commentary]
said appreciatively
"Look at your hair—
it's all
soft and smooth
and behaving itself"—
Oh!
Sucker: vindicated.
Triumphantly laurelled
in the sun-glowing
fluffy
Marianne Faithfull hair
she's longed for,
ever
this sucker.

[Erg]

I can't even look at the man
who brings in his travel mug
the size of a moonshine jug
to fill with coffee
though our sign clearly states
that 75-cent refills
may not exceed 16 ounces.
If I look at him
grit-on-edge go the teeth
and up goes the irrational blood pressure
and that will never do
as our medical insurance
is weak
and our dental insurance
nonexistent.

[Snarl]

I can get all
[secretly]
[and perhaps unduly]
whipped up at the coffee stand
when people ram the
half-and-half carafe at me
demanding that I refill it.
At such times
capable
of but one single thought:
"Oh good Lord.
Be a man.
If you're going to drink coffee,
then drink your coffee
you milky milk-toast milkmaid"
and perhaps that is
unkind
unchristian
and lazy of me

but I prefer it black.

[Postulate:

Man + Guitar → Sex!!]

I don't know why it's true
but it damn well is
My counselor [bass player] husband
has a vague Freudian theory
but it's perfectly cliché
and besides
most of his Freud is rusty
he says.

But I cannot resolve my feelings
toward Graham Nash
who *abandoned* his group
    [and his wife!
      and his homeland!
        and how many kids I don't know!
Were they invited along?
If not, then HEX!!!
as I am big on families.
Mostly.
When I'm not being bitter
about the padlocked womb.]
but he *came* to America
and *much* was happening
an artist—a driven man—
the art it *drives* you
[oh I hate myself for defending him

oh Rose! Volatile waitress
I sympathize
Volatile myself on occasion.]

[although as artist
showing your creation to those too close
can be a hideous freak-out
like stripping naked
pale/flabby/hairs in the wrong places
the head aches afterward
oh please love it I wish to dazzle you
I often fail to dazzle my husband with poetry
it seems to work better when they don't
know you all *through* inside]

and his GROUP
WHY didn't they want to say more
to mean more?
It seems they did want to
but only after he'd left
A strange sad fizzling
could be heard amid the harmonies
but they wanted to go on being English
and for that who could blame them?
What happened?
What's the story?
Why has no one written it?
[There's probably a biography out there in Swedish]
Dammit they'll mess around & die

and then we'll never know

And could be it was better
for them to dwindle
[although Tony Hicks evolving
into rock god
might have been worth cherishing]
[in its way]
[no perhaps it's better like this]
[is it? Would it? Heh?]
[yes. No. no--yes. No. ?]
[damned irresistible nature of rock & roll...]

In the end, Graham, you hippie twit,
you were a man with a guitar
and nothing can fix that.
The same sad ache
with which the belly-dancer
crippled you
in New York 1965
plagued the devotees of your group
so that
in moments of high harmonies
and brilliant musical execution
they would've scaled high and slick walls
in their go-go boots
to but
[beatnik goatee be hanged]
kiss your lips

and rub noses

just for the barest instant.

Even I feel that way

and you're probably not my type at all.

[Skyloft Realm]

We're indoorsy I'm afraid
and out back the swing set
is ghostly beyond all reason in the wind
Today meeting the boy at the bus stop
grey clouds sat—thunk—
dark steely shelves in sky
and I pointed them out to him
"Look how cool the clouds are."
He said "Yes I know. And
I saw little bright flashes
in them and I think it
means people died.
I don't know if that's true
but I think so."
And I declared it a sound
and intriguing theory.

[French Smack]

Tonight the gals discuss *The Paris Wife*
and my contribution is Le Marquis
[Chocolate Spongecake] from
Mastering the Art of French Cooking
Julia Child never having failed me not once
and while baking it
blared
Pop à Paris *Rock 'n' Roll & Miniskirts*
Compilation 2
and four Hollies songs
sung in French
and how did I get to Feb 2012
never having heard the Hollies
sing in French?
Up they go
to the top of my list of French Exceptions
[which is to say]
the French language rankles me
except in the following cases:

1. The Hollies
2. Paul McCartney
3. little children
4. my graphic-novel character with the dead, French mother so that he lapses into French-speak at times of illness, exhaustion and crisis and resembles the pizza boy of my youth

    5.   Donovan Leitch

    6.   Pop à Paris *Rock 'n' Roll & Miniskirts Compilation 2*

I don't like French and the above exceptions

prove it unbearable I suppose...

My French consists of some

half-dozen words

and the lyrics to *Michelle*

so I am ill-equipped to judge the Hollies

regarding their accents.

But I assume they're perfect.

[Gratitude & Baditude]

If that "bit of extra" at my middle
isn't JELLY enough
then I'm scared it's packed with tumors.
It happened once before
13 years ago
Lucky or unlucky?
Verdict life in the end
but still
took with 'em most of my eggs
and ambitions of rampant babymaking
but as the beats say
Life is not without its acids
The raspberry Jell-O with milk
it must be hard won.

[Frazzled Deacon Pushes Envelope]

The old man tense with work all week
the rages and turmoils and lies
and hyperactive abused children of strangers
why
they do take their toll
so it's to Springfield with him
on Sunday
where he and his pal
will tweak the family guitars
switch pickups
swap out strings
"raise the action" here and there
and fiddle around inside of amplifiers
to keep the mind straight and level
and the boy and I stay behind
in the warm bliss of freezer pizza
and woodfire and no car.
Our boy age six
guilty with the thrill of skipping church
rapidly twines and untwines fingers
chanting
I still love God
I still love God
I still love God.

[My main man]

Up early on a Saturday
he'd kept the coals going all night
in the stove
and threw on a log in the morning
to leave us a good fire
before taking the car for an
oil-change

All that's him telling us
we matter the most

that

we're the cold stupid def dope
as the kids said back in my day.

[Les visages des petits enfants]

It's a Hollies song
sung in French
but don't leave it there.
It's April days in
black turtlenecks and
beat-striped crewnecks
3 round the microphone
and a language coach
spicy aftershave
and agony of inflection
gut-pitting flashes of school-room
twining vocals
harmonies creeping climbing as ivies
nearly dark now
let's get it over
Part of the day-job
is bestowing on
foreign fans
a beloved song in their own language
through sweaty industry
The song has been old to me since
1987 [age 12 babysitting sang it to a little girl when she cried]
But now [2012! Flying cars! Or so we had imagined...]
it's an entirely new song
and I'm young and fawning again
energized
silky all over and rapt.

[Feb 25]

No please winter
don't go
I need the woodfires if I'm to be
kind
I need these walls and roof
for safety and obscurity
This spring we'll consume
copious bowls of
Raspberry Jell-O with Milk
What was it, Mr. Romo?
Raspberry Jell-O *made* with milk?
Or regular, prepared, water-based
raspberry Jell-O cubed and *mixed* with milk?
It's the former,
to my way of thinking
and yes
Raspberry Jell-O with Milk
The spring will be endurable
if we have that.

[Ce dulce]

G7sus4
is code for a thing I need
to play a Bob Dylan song
[he's not usually my scene but sometimes yes
occasionally yes will crawl inside of a song of his
and live for a week]
and the "sus"
is for "suspended"
but I always slip and
pronounce it "soos"
Gee-seven-soos-four
having lived in Romania one
long-ago winter
prior to my guitar days
and *sus* is "soos"
meaning up
or upstairs
or high.

[Hem v. Nash]

Friday *Paris Wife*
book discussion
crawling with church gals
all save one
but she too
very much affronted
at Hemingway's philandering
and I the wildly jealous type
even so heard my own voice
defending the rat
the Art!
the Times!
Experience!
Kill a bull!
Take a mistress.
It was Graham Nash all over again
all absinthe
flappers & hippies
& art & jazz
      & fashions
           & passions
               & flowers
                    & guitars
& the room hot
with church-gal protest
[though Bex gave me a nod]
and what was it

about those fired- up holy church gals

[100% correct]

made me want

to escort them

to the dark side?

[Noel Gallagher Dream!]

So there we sat
around a table
in the English equivalent of
a Mega-lo-Mart
in a glass-enclosed office
overlooking trees and castles.
Noel Gallagher
was attempting to
buy back his Union Jack guitar
(into which he'd carved
cryptic messages)
from Scandinavian thieves,
but the asking price
was too high.
Thinking of it now,
why didn't he just kick
their asses?
I couldn't take my eyes away
as he pulled money
(American bills)
from the pocket of his jeans
and shook his head
so smoky
so human.
My old school chum Scott R
and I sat by,
laughing
at funny English television commercials
including one with a
white-haired lady
having a meal in her garden,
wielding a bottle of
orange salad dressing
called "Carrot Glacé"

Anyway, Sally was just drifting into the fantasy where she & Noel Gallagher ~~people~~ sing "Baby, It's Cold Outside"...

[So Casual regarding Miracles]

Perched at coffee stand
my doula walks past
We shared an intimate fourteen hours
six years ago

We should be sharing a pot of tea now
across pink roses in bone china
and serene knowing low-lidded nods
over secrets of the world and all time

but there she goes

having seen me stark-naked
flushed and bloody
having braided my hair
and rescued me
from the point where
pushing out a 9-lb.-12-oz. baby
was suddenly too searing and mortal
and exhausting

saved me
with reports of
his newly-visible
full head of hair.

[Confrontation]

There was protest art on Friday
with Teachers' Meetings having
closed down the schools
and the boy taking into his head
that I should be home
from work at 10:12 a.m.
instead of 10:15
scrawled on his palm
in *permanent*
red Sharpie marker:

> I wish
> that you
> would
> cum home

[he spelled 'would' right
after conferring with his dad]
then slammed into his room.
When I came home
emerged all lit up smiling
but remembered himself
sulked
just long enough
to present me
with the message
like a traffic cop.

[The Nervous Type]

The boy feels it all too
sharply
and I love that about him
One particular
grueling [video game] battle
between his father
and a wicked terrifying tentacled monster
left the lad with headache
and upset stomach
so that I tucked him under
the Hungarian goose down
of [what ends each night as]
the Family Bed
fed him peppermint
and left him to watch
Peep cartoons on my iPod.
He is a little Novalis
and I am so relieved
because if he had gone in for football
what then?
Whatever would we talk about?

[Split Music Festival 1968]

When that scene was happening
I was nowhere.
I was an egg
inside of a
lonely well-dressed young girl
in a gloomy marriage
in Clayton-Ladue
a rich St. Louis neighborhood

and an unformed sperm
in a southern-Missouri college
Doors-style rock band
[guitar and organ].

Strange I feel so at home there.

"Get your own scene"
balk the elders
scold other people's parents
[where mine just liked
to see me enjoy life and its music]
and there *was* a scene
somewhere
miles off
London
        Manchester
                drug-addled

sick & unfortunate
        too fortunate
damaged   outraged
slightly less fashionable
and hateful no end.

[Mistress of Faded Beauty]

The Skyward Sword video game
that came at Christmas
well
he's played 152 hours
and is sick of it now.
So I whip the *Metroland* metaphor on him:
"Oh no!
She's slurping her tea
and patting her lips dry
with her long hair
after every sip
and you've noticed now
and it makes you sneer!"
but the metaphor goes right on past him
I suppose he hasn't seen that movie
or read that book
so I'm alone again
in the white bathroom
a bit niggled
that maybe
such *Metroland*-spouting
is equivalent to tea-slurping
and using one's long hair
as serviette.

[Crisco {Ode}]

So I was recruited by church gals
to teach a pie-crust seminar
at a ladies' get-together
and planning supplies I suggested Crisco
to keep things simple and cheap
and the planners made a note of it.

[Also, it's what my great-grandmother used...]

Then musing aloud I mentioned that
the butter-and-lard combo is nice
for its workability and flakiness
the Crisco crust a flaky champion
you'll kill 'em at the county fair
but you have to roll it out between sheets of waxed paper.

And one gal pointed out that the ladies might prefer lard-and-butter
what with their distrust of packaged items such as Crisco
and immediately
my inward gargoyle uncurled rubbed its eyes grew unsightly horns
and soured up at the church ladies
[who habitually outstrip me in childbearing]
and their smug health-food habits
which I once shared [practically invented]
until it didn't get me any more babies
then what was the point
throwing down piles of cash
and chasing all over town for organic?

Davy Jones himself a vegetarian & a jogger
dead at 66
heart attack
just last week
and did Maureen McCormick wince at all?
Anyhow
the subject changed over to home-baked cookies
Laura very adamant about one strict and perfect texture

but down on Crisco as a rule.
Crispy! she kept saying
until I countered with my preference for chewy
and she confused me then saying it must be *both*.

Well, let's look at these ones I made yesterday
said I
and fetched the yellow-glazed crock
to show her the chocolate-chip spice cookies
and she took one saying
Yes.
Look at the beautiful.
Look at the beautiful.
So that I felt compelled to point out—
Crisco.

To sit in the presence of God
To sit in the presence of God
To sit in the presence of God
To sit in the presence of God
To sit in the presence of God
I want to I
want to
I want to want to.

[Poem. For Bass Players.]

Would SOMEBODY
dammit
write a biography
of John Entwistle?
The guy at the library said he would
--the first in a long line
of bass-player bios,
he vowed
And I said OH--
not to belittle your hard work
but could you sell them for
five or ten bucks apiece
and could they be
available everywhere
like at gas stations
and grocery stores
so that I could
you know
pick one up on a Friday
with my black chocolate bars
and clove cigarettes
and diet cherry cola
and make it a weekend
a luscious weekend of
acquired knowledge
of excellently-sideburned troubled geniuses
to burrow and reside
in a small corner of my half-doomed soul
among the candy-colored
satin pillows
all over the bed?

[Hypothetical Spousal Confab]

Wife: Sunshine would you please go do prayers with the boy while I get this pie out?

Husband: ...

Husband: ...

Wife: SUNSHINE WILL YOU PLEASE DO PRAYERS WITH THE BOY YES OR NO??

Husband: (defensive) (and still just sitting there) I *thought* it was *assumed* I *would.*

Wife: ...

Wife: (internally) Well. That is the most asinine thing I have ever heard and now I'm off to fantasize about a young Tony Hicks, hair circa 1967.

In black and white and grey as in the films of the time.

Not terribly talkative as in a gelatin print.

He has it much easier than the old man, really.

No expectations of him only to say it with guitar and quiet whispers.

As on acetate.

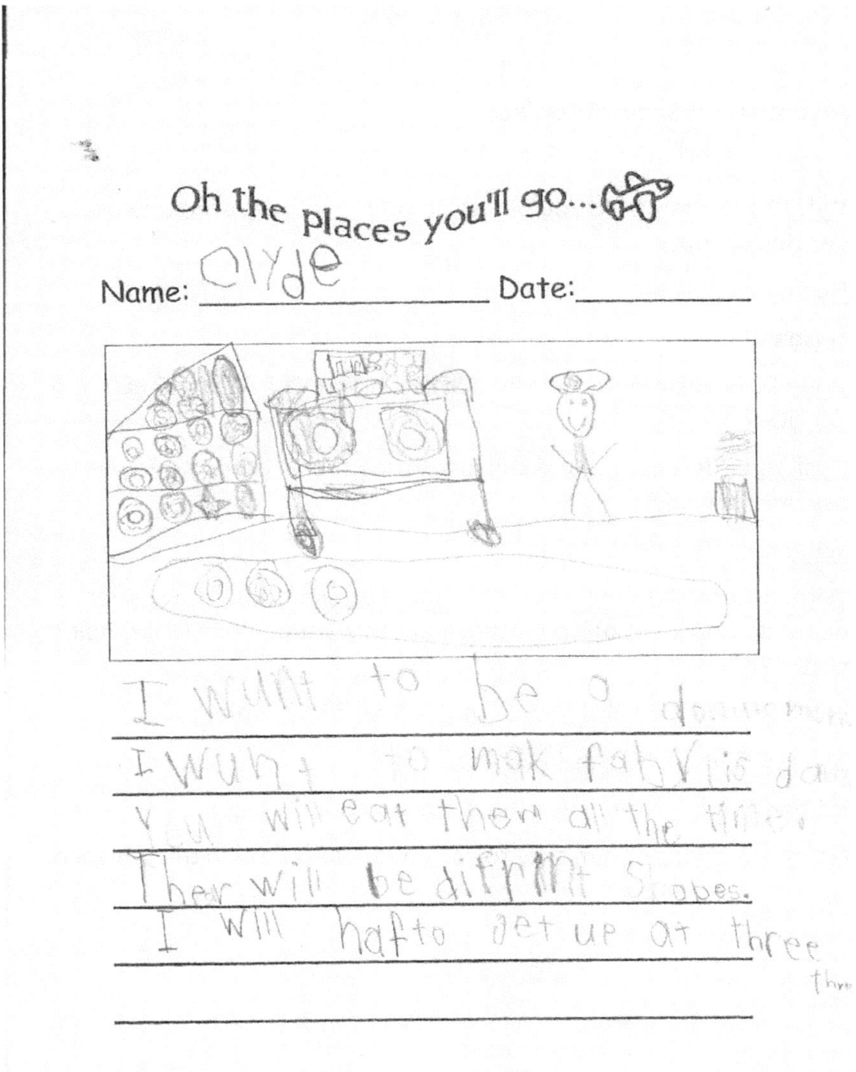

Figure 1

Kindergarten Essay: *I wunt to be a donuts makr. I wunt to mak fabvlis donuts. You will eat them all the time. Thear will be difrint shapes. I will haf to get up at three thrty.*
--Our Clyde age 6, Feb. 2012

[Monday Morning all Gritty and Real!]

I rose to the occasion
here in the real world
and said 'Good morning'
to the elderly gent
who volunteers shelving fiction
in the library
Mondays.
Might rather have
stayed alone
up in my head
early morning
but then
who dying
ever says
'I wish I'd spent more
time in fantasy'?

[She's Right I Do Like to Feed People]

After church we fed ten people
[counting us]
with beef stew
biscuits and cake
and all of my social misgivings aside
I always feel warm at home
as hostess
and well settled afterward.
And come to think of it
my mind recalls
the voice of my main man
as I flitted after cups and bowls
in kitchen
telling the whole company
how they would love my beef stew
he'd never cared for beef stew
before I came along
but mad for it now.

[a kindness to remember when vexed]

[Making Ready a Little]

Clyde will break our hearts one day
and jet off to Amsterdam or Stockholm
to be a painter or pastry chef
and leave us as 2 dry sockets
after wisdom-tooth surgery
Our only child plucked and cut away
For now
his need for us
is as desperate
as every other emotion he encounters
deep
        ripping
                steeped in longing
                        wrapped with ache
and mothering him is so often
honey and wine
my engorged stockpiles
of care and nurturing
at last given vent.
But fathering him
bleeds one pale
who never felt the night
as smothering terror
or found no torment in possibility of
school bus never arriving to take you home
or hasn't known exploding panic
at thoughts of ghosts and thunderstorms and wasps

but who now does recognize
that when the boy has left us
the hole will throb.

[Back When Invincible]

Tornadoes scare the hell out of me
but used to be they didn't
[survived one
two blocks from granddad's house
age 8 in the cupboard with mom & sister
cousins in closet crazy menfolk outside watching
the newspaper photo looked like lightning]
indeed I rather hoped for them in high school
signaling fresh wet hormonal springtime
the strong smell of the Lipton tea plant
just hanging there thick
and all to the basement
milling & banter
too cool to duck & cover
Chance encounters
one hoped
with beautiful green-eyed trombone-player
or the sweet smirking fellow from the drum line
[dead at 19 car accident]
or that odd, sleepy-eyed cross-country runner
once seen army-crawling into the little gym
one night after a basketball game.
I never figured that one out
but now suspect Mad Dog liquor.

[Unsolicited Beauty Secret]

At coffee kiosk played bartender
to 83-yr-old woman
        who said
if she had it to do over
she would only
take better care of her skin
but never could abide
the feel of cream on her face
still can't
and was very outdoorsy
the windier the better!
I did the math in my little notebook
She was born 1928 or '29
and used to visit neighbor ladies
with 'faces like nuns'
when she was a girl
would go into their house
and once in the kitchen
learned their secret
which was olive oil
        warmed on the stove
        and massaged into the skin
and of course
they never went outside
again she said
they lived like nuns.
No kids to play with
No garden to speak of.

[Thoughts on Wherewithal]

I envied the calm certainty
of that rural chick
five years ago
all cloaked and swimming in
PURPOSE and
      WORTH
mothered eight children
and described how
her mornings
MUST follow a
certain sort of
clockwork
"I put on the oat-mill
[oatmeal]
then iron my husband's shirt..."
The vicious inward atom
spirals erratically
& proclaims
I could have been so
worthwhile as she
if only I'd gone on having babies
The crippling sticky-brained
melancholy
only arrived when I couldn't
With no time for introspection
and all days full of
jelly pies
maple-tinged corn mush
sock puppets behind the couch
and storybooks in wildflowers
I could have done it.
Couldn't I?
Could I?
I wouldn't have
driven them
into the river
would I?

[Lovergirl]

Some type of female peak
is going on inside of me
and for that everything on the planet is sexy.
Elderly men in the library smelling of bay rum
Sexy
I can see them as they were in past
tall and virile
in hats.
Men in western movies
Sexy
Even the comical dopey ones
their eyes just thunder at me.
Aged beat musicians
who knew how to smolder
in youthful photographs
Devastating
in their jackets and sunglasses
peering around corners
and the whole point of all of this is
a human body's last-ditch
effort to make one last baby
That part of me doesn't work anymore
but strangely
some other part of me
doesn't know that—
a little tiny bit remindful of
a baby dying shortly after birth
and milk coming into the breasts anyhow
—but actually forgive me
it's not like that at all
as some sensations in this time
in spite of loss
are terribly enjoyable
                wonderfully
                      madly
                              smashingly
                                      enjoyable.

[Consider the following Tactic]

So's your old man.

I really must
use that more often
to defuse arguments.

I mean—to stop myself
shooting my mouth off

Or perhaps a signal:
'You know I'm the ludicrously sensitive type, pally,
and that remark stung!'

In action:

Husband: There's not
enough ice
in my cup.

Wife: So's your old man.

[Tub Scrub Remix]

Always scrub your own bathroom
if vulnerable to mentalities.
Scrub the bathroom
Scrub the bath
Clean the toilet
Wash the floor
Scrub
Scrub the bathroom
or the crazy will get you.

So then
Brimful of laudable scouring ambitions
but interrupted
by evidence
of husband performing
Farmer's Hanky in shower.
Blech!!
Times were when both of us young & lovely
I'd've reacted:
Oh! Poor booger.
Poor sweet human soul gone clotty & bewildered
with rubberized snot
and had to expel it
dear love
Now almost eleven years in
and acquainted with his fussiness
and scarce initiative at birthdays
it's BLECH!!
and disdain for his sluggy nose-turds.

No picnic myself as life-mate of course
only just having snarled at him
for being underfoot and
alerted to the sin of it
while listening to broody old pop groups
lowing and cooing to some horrid shrew
about what a peach his new gal is

she treats him nice
does everything for him
carves out time for him
now here I go climbing
into the toilet where I belong
and scrub like hell.

[Ironing, Contemplative]

In days before Permanent Press
ironing was a drudge I suppose
but then
as with cigarettes and certain
guitar-chord progressions
providing me kinship
with pop stars of old,
when age 14 or 15
I hounded my mother
to teach me to iron men's shirts
and pressed my services
onto babysitting clients
whose ironing had piled up
in the laundry room
[no extra charge]

partly for the glad & wholesome
connection to the midcentury housewife

but also erotic somehow
smoothing with heat
the fabric
that will touch a man's skin
through his workday

and the sensual wife of

the sultry & necktied

anonymous jazz drummer

mid-1960's

in search of soothing answer

to aching absence-fondness

amid long tours

might try

ironing all of his shirts at once

with records playing

ending up clad only

in one of the

new-pressed garments

and panties

caught reveling

in sex and beat music

by mother-in-law

at the back door.

[Bus Stop Wig-Out]

Earl Grey my sweet
protect me should it rain
The boy's bus late maybe
he'll cry
forgot my phone
what time is it
Is his teacher calling?
I'll never get another cigarette lit in this wind
One cigarette
is all you get
A clove one equals five
they say
Five cigarettes
is all you get in a school day
Oh here the bus comes
Thank God.

[To remember the cold when old]

The miserable thing about the death of winters
is the fond backward glance
at beat musicians
every single group with its
black-and-white films
of playing songs outdoors all bundled up
in wool coats
and furs
mad furs
and steaming breath
blowing hair
frigid fingers
locking up along guitar strings
and the occasional keyboard
all of it
slicing at the budding mother-hearts
of teen girls prompting them
to hone tea-brewing skills once home
always British Isles or Scandinavia
reliably cold the weather
and if the others were only agreeable
for two cents I'd relocate there
or to Iceland or Alaska
and film pop bands out in the cold
in hand-knit scarves
and star-quality imitation-badger coats
prolong the primal blessedness
of ice and woodfires
home-baked bread
and steamy-breathed songsters
before the whole planet boils
and we evacuate in rocketships.

[Death and Old Things]

Friday around
3:15 in the afternoon
walked out of the Antique Shop
and across the street
at the graveyard heard a 21-gun salute.

In the shop heard
songs I hadn't
heard since high school
and they were
old songs even then

Was after an extra
blade-type pastry cutter or two
for the pie-crust seminar tomorrow
no luck
only the wire-type
how can there be
kitchen mojo
in even a dead
woman's pastry cutter
if it's the WIRE kind?

Besides
it cost twice as much
as the same malarkey
at Wal-Mart

Did find however
a real boss cake comb
with swirly-green

Bakelite handle
five bucks

in fact
everything I found was green—
fortuitous in March—

Jade-ite coffee cup
three dollars

and *Parade of Stories*
a 1965 storybook for the kid
a buck-fifty and like new

but most of all
I've always meant
since a bride
to own a cake comb
with a Bakelite handle
though I never make
angel food cake
[what do you do with
all of those leftover egg yolks
except mountains of laborious custard?]
and chiffon cake only seldom

but nevertheless
important
certainly
for kitchen mojo
and also now
a murder weapon

in a story I'm doing.

Would have liked
a bit of the Vaseline glass
—glows green under blacklight!
but only
coasters
a juicer
cream-and-sugar set
no ashtray.

Death
all up in smoke
Life
A breath exhaling smoke

After all.

[Last Cold Night on Earth]

The gin kicked in nicely and the gibberish flowed
Beatific lethargy giving way
to all manner of lovemaking uninhibited
all naked amid blazing stove-fire

last cool day probably forever
so we overdid it
kept throwing logs on

Stripped
        sipped
                slid off the couch languid

disturbingly
through the giddy fog
my voice sounded to me
much like that of my mother
with dementia
low & deep & muttery

not that she would rattle on tipsy about
the fellow on "Marple" looking SO like
Colin Blunstone of the Zombies
that it must be his love-child
and say!
do the credits mention a BLUNSTONE
or was it his anonymous love-child?

Mother would never say *that*
she never much cared for the Zombies
and with her you can't
understand the words anymore
and she'll get stuck on the
last syllable
like a record-player hitting a deep scratch

but vocally

we were
last night
the same woman

[the old man didn't seem to notice
and fearing it would kill the sex
I kept my mouth shut about it.]

[Hell with your Bagel]

Today
coffee kiosk
and time will crawl
heart stubbornly remiss
in its care for your scone
My little'n
home with fever
99.8 at 7:30 a.m.
then 100-point-*something*
what was it?

His dad told me
on the phone at 9:45

If I'm not there to worry him well,
how will it come about then?

It's true though.
He won't drink
the chamomile-vanilla-ginger-honey tea
if I don't REMIND him

I never know with fevers
when is the right time to panic

You hear of deaths occasionally

and from 2-8
I won't have the car
should he take an awful turn

and was it our
gin-spattered
beer-splashed
love-soaked

stove-blazing

heating the house
up to 79⁰ last night

what done it?

[Reality! Full-blast]

You know he feels lousy
and it's gone to his stomach
whenever he peeps feebly,
"Will I die?"
Such is his pattern
Savor the fever one whole day
and then with the faltering gut
and the death-brooding
Ohh...*honey*
you won't die
[and
too
get ready with the sick bowl].

[Revivification]

Our boy so spindly after 3-day illness
"Poor little lamb needs pie"
was all I could say

[Last week being a heavy one for pie
3 pies for ladies' retreat
1 for father-in-law's birthday
& 3 pie-crust tutorials]

He expects
once he's climbed off the school-bus
that I'll have made him a pie
and he's right.
I will have.
Twin Peaks Cherry
with Cool Whip.

[So Act Surprised]

I've planned Christmas—
big jars of peaches in brandy
[we'll can 'em in summer
when the Amish have fine peaches]
and copies of *Darling* on DVD.
In the film they nicked their peaches
from Harrod's
and no one will approve
but some may appreciate
the eye-grabbing
mouth-watering
drama & scandal
and the peaches
will be loved by some
and held strange by others
mysterious and weird
as if we'd given them a jar full of baby.

[The Eye of Tony Hicks]

The right grey eye of Tony Hicks
hangs arty on the bulletin board
in my bathroom
like a muse to cajole the verse, prose
clothing construction
and guitar-practice
and to conceal my words
should a guest need our spare toilet.

Missouri folklore holds
that the soul of a depraved
French pop star
was condemned to a portrait
on a bathroom wall
captive to gawk upon
private eliminations
imperfect nakedness
removal of unwanted hair
and vomiting

but Tony doesn't mind
He's just an eye
A carefully posed and terribly English
eyeball
on paper
so none of it troubles him.

Nor that fellow from the Troggs
[a head and some shoulders]
And same goes for the Swedish model
up to whom he cozies
She is one paint-lined brown eye
with gorgeous lashes
and he can smell nothing but her perfume.

From the bathtub I catch the reflection
of their eyes in the mirror

exactly as seen by themselves
years ago
except not in color

Like them
I've only seen the outward
real-life
unreflected versions in photographs

Even so
most of the horrors round here
occur in the other bathroom
the illnesses and clogs
and one might be heard
to report to the eyes now and again
'Only be glad you got the
fluffy-white
daisy-scented
girly bathroom, hey?'

[Cuss the Sky]

81º mid-March
[*Ides* of March]
not even St. Patrick's Day and
81 crummy hateful ass-melting
degrees

Warm weather always
a torturous leap anyway
therefore necessary
to remember
sun tea
and to plot schemes

"Slide guitar,"
my husband nodded
"We'll spend the evenings
on the back porch learning it"
and wonderful
that idea hit the mark exactly

So then
the summer project
is slide guitar on back deck
& strict regime of
Elmore James
Slim Harpo
the Doors
Jell-O salads
Ronnie Dawson
Eddie Cochran
homemade sodapop
strawberry shortcake
herb garden
lemon-balm tea
peanut butter pie
Western movies

Be *American*
[damn you]

though I cling
to my British treasures
and pray
for a cold, cold
April.

[Graveyard Walks]

Once for a week last spring
I took morning walks in the vast old cemetery
two doors down from my library job.

And people seemed to live a long time in this town
the last couple of centuries
at least along the main paths

But anyhow

I stopped the cemetery walks
because that Friday
my legs got tangled in a fishing line
strewn far and wide over various headstones
and across pathways
and I feared
that the cemetery manager's son
[Purple Heart in Vietnam]
was the suspicious sort   and
mistaking me for a no-good vandal
had set a trap for me.

Why else would fishing line
be all over a graveyard
in the middle of town?

[Crossing Guard—I]

What are the crossing-guard's
plans after work?
I assume they're pleasant
and envy her
but that is always the way.
A peaceful Pepsi with Maury Povich
or whatever's the talk-show they like now
The true-crime stylings of Ann Rule
simple contentment
neighbors
swinging by for chat
and orange pop
in big plastic bottles
and Town House Crackers
and onion dip
Lo.
Oprah's on.

[Crossing Guard—II]

My grandmother
was a crossing-guard
once

on duty 1963 or so
when an impulsive
6-year-old girl
shot out into the street
and was killed by a car

tragic local scandal

investigation
eventually
cleared my grandma

The girl was buried
in her father's plot
in the veterans' cemetery
there in Springfield
and later he joined her
in the same grave.

[Too Many Rules for New Life]

What of it, Friday?
Where's my Zombies bio
and why is my tongue all fuzzy-coated?
Hopefully a mere matter of
all of my Wu-violations
and not of catching boy's illness
what with company coming tomorrow
my sister & her gang
and Mediterranean food
I would hate to miss!
I tried to brush away the tongue-scum
but the toothpaste turned it
an unsettling oceany green
and I should explain what is a Wu-violation.

Wu is a Chinese doctor out in LA
& twice briefly I relied upon her Chinese wisdom in a book
trying a second time to get pregnant

She says to make a welcome womb for a new life
the body must be neither too hot nor too cold
and also not too damp
and the way to control this is
eating certain foods
and avoiding others
but first
identify your current constitution
[mine tending toward too warm
tongue fuzz a symptom
I've got the fever
I'm hot
I can't be stopped]
Exacerbating the too-warm by heating further
would be caffeine
such as in coffee
[had that today]
and cola

[had that]
and carrots I believe
[as it takes a lot of red-hot energy
to digest their fibrous little hides
and I ate a pile of them at lunch]
and uncooked wild garlic
[had that in the hummus]
and cigarettes probably
[I'm having one now]

and also it's ass-vexingly hot out
[oh wait *there's* a nice breeze]

Cooled it with greens
and one meager gulp of green tea
but otherwise a big ol'
Wu-scandal
here today inside of me
as if I shunned new life altogether
which I only do because
it's apparently none of my business
and striving to welcome it
makes me horrible
panicked
and boring
the hope and the vice-dodging
being quite draining and all.

Of course the dad is invited
to eat a soup of seahorse
[the only male on the planet that gives birth]
but I would never ask him to.
Bizarre foods send him straight to Panicsville
He would be traumatized
and hate the hypothetical child
ever after possibly

But the real truth seems to be
I should have taken up smoking years ago

and tacked on excessive drinking
and other recreationals
after the example of so many
soaked and drug-sodden rock stars
and arty types
siring seven children apiece
so that you realize
that justice is being furtive and coy again
and you're damned sick of chasing it.

As for the Wu plan
I kicked it to the curb
long ago
but still occasionally
dream in its language.

[Baker's Despair]

Glorious-apt-and-comforting
Pistol-shooting analogy
from husband
upon the falling of my
hot-milk sponge cakes
[two round golden layers
sucking lemons!!]
and my consequent cussing rampage—
The perfect score in pistol-shooting is 1700
I think
and in 1974
      the year of my birth
some man got within 24 points
      and no one's ever touched him.
In fact
what everyone aims for is 1600
which is considered
pretty damned whippy
like the four-minute mile
so the point is
      once in a while
           cakes fall
the bastards
and the day before Cake Club too
[We no longer call it Book Club
after five years we've stopped kidding ourselves
too irresponsible to read whole boring bestsellers
too stubborn and tired to cross over
to one another's vampire novels
fantasy tomes
and Brit-Pop biographies
Let's just eat cake together]
So what have you got for me, Dinah Shore?
Your fudge cake an absolute cinch
and orgiastic in the mouth
but square and dowdy
And being drunk with pride

and love for the gals
I wanted to treat 'em nice
with a big round-tall-and-swirly
American layered affair
But running out of baking powder mid-cake
dashing to Moser's grocery
batter in fridge meantime
and hot milk allowed to cool
plus peeking in the oven halfway through
wrecked my afternoon's efforts.
Still.
We're a mildly broken crew
and therefore
appreciative
of any cake
that may come our way.

In the end a two-layer
[beauteous, unfallen]
chocolate cake
with Vanilla Buttercream
Vile Temptress from the pages of
Cook's Illustrated's pretty little volume
How to Make an American Layer Cake, 1997
[There. See? True patriotism to say I adore you.]

and one *could* wax all naughty
drawing racy parallels
between the American Layer Cake
and what goes on in the bedroom
See the base layer
recumbent
submissive
tender-crumbed
and ready for love...

But hey.
Next time.

[Spring Exhibition]

Two rabbits doing it in the front yard
[my husband announced & I came running]
"There. By Skipper's van," he said,
giving the next-door neighbors' dog
ownership of the family vehicle
and we stared out the window
but they'd finished
by that time
and just crouched
nose-to-nose
and didn't care
who could see 'em.

[Tragödie]

My feelings are gone!
I don't have feelings anymore!
You hurt them so bad they died!
[said my 6-year-old kid when
I sent him to bed for throwing tantrums]
You killed my feelings.
All of them.
They died.
I don't feel anything.

{So then you won't feel sad if all of your Legos disappear...?}

My feelings came back.
They died and came back and died again.

{They've had a hard day.}

[The Bobby Elliott Corollary]

It's a real wicked hat
Bob.
But that isn't the point.

It's the stunning jumble
of British teeth
that courts my frivolity.
It's your carefully-maintained
Northern way of speaking
which brings on the
undignified sighs.

It's how many drives
age 16
down Selsa Road
Independence, Missouri
caught tangled in
one of your drum fills
half-collapsed
in teenaged dramatic fashion
over the steering wheel
breathless
"Oh please drummer
I just can't—"

To this day
certain of your fills
sneak up and get handsy.

Selsa Road all spectral
in front of my eyes.

[Squirm and Wince]

Carl Perkins my dear one
Spring has come
So just you leave the light on
& I'll happily get Dixie-fried with you.
And I'll bring the cake.
I'm hard-pressed to muster up
the necessary indifference toward England
but spring has come
and apologies to the health-conscious
but fixing dessert pies
and fruit cobblers and pandowdies
and round cakes all filled
and tarted up in gowns of silky frosting
[all to the tune of my native rockabilly]
is my best hope for reclaiming
my American guts and livers
and for loving the lilac'ed land
God gave me
now spring has come.

[The Painful Changeover]

Bless your soul lemon balm
So great was my shame
at shunning the springtime when
[of all things] pop songs
suddenly reminded me that spring's coming
was ever a great relief in olden times
when winter was more of a killer

My horny-handed girl-of-the-soil days
just meshed too profoundly
with my young-mother days
when poor fertility of soil
mirrored
poor fertility of womb
and my little lad ached me
by outgrowing his shoes
and outgrowing them again.

At Thanksgiving
abandoned the garden
untidily snubbed dead cornstalks and
pumpkin vines
left the last turnips to toughen and bolt
too bitter for Italian soup
failed utterly to protect her in any fashion
no mulch
newspapers or tarps
just lolled in winter's bed
and cuddled up to him like a whore
wearing nothing but a lipstick-sneer
and a filthy satin slip
flushed all over with stove-heat.

[And a glorious affair it was
all holed up
with electric guitars
books of poetry

and record-players
like college
but less responsible]

Now in spite of my rebellious indoorsy dallying
and my beautiful useless negligent winter
of woodfire
Gimlets
beat music
and Rod Serling,
we have greening out back
onions garlic lavender
heaps of sage
3 strawberry plants
spreading blackberry vines and
[our momentary absence of stomach-ache
and throat ailment aside]
lemon balm!
You came back anyway.

[Sally Has a Kitchen Disaster!]

It's a painting in Detroit
and a mom-band rock album
 in Detroit
and being a beautiful phrase
it's the one I employ
to announce kitchen disasters of my own.

Sally had a kitchen disaster
Wednesday
Having scrubbed the roots for dandelion coffee
absent-mindedly stuffed leaves and stems
down garbage disposal
and clogged the u-pipes
but fixed it rather easily
and should that hippie in the herb-book
be correct in her leanings
toward the sweetness of spring-dandelion coffee
thankfully
very little sweetness was lost in the process.

[Precious {Rock} Moments]

Not only is the boy singing himself to sleep
with the singsong slogan "Mr. Mojo Risin'"
he also announced that when the
substitute kindergarten teacher
asked for a Z-word today
he gave her "Zeppelin"
as in Led
[he confirmed]
rather than
dirigibles
in general.

[Thoughts on Motoring]

Nowadays when an aged gentleman
swoops out in front of you with his car
cuts you off and drives terribly
you can still kind of say
Well maybe he was in the War
We can't be *too* hard on him.
But once it's baby boomers
or Generation X out there
old
with driving skills corroded
slow & creaky & rude
unless the pendulum of good-nature swings back a ways
the young folk will possibly assume we're assholes
and just ram us on into the Sweet By-and-By.

[To the Elementary School Bus Driver]

Oh shattered bus lady
it can't possibly matter to you
the price I pay every time
you're late to the grade-school
afternoons
Haven't you read the previous pages
in reference to my 3-ft.-9-inch Novalis
who pales and weeps in the face of such catastrophe?
Pales and weeps and
climbs off the bus cheeks stained
with tears and magic-marker
shudders to attend school next 3 days
knowing his mother is stranded carless
unable to rescue
and the dismal vision curls around him
convinced of his doom
in fact
to reside at the school
the rest of his days
nights all bats and ghouls and dead black tree-limbs
grasping through terribly lonely fogs.
I imagine you
bus lady
being late because your old man belted you one
and stitches were required
or something to do with securing a bail bond
for someone
or lingering over cigarettes and paralyzing indifference.

[Oh, Expletive]

Listed among the sins
of the deep dark inward places
are sensuality
foolishness
coveting
pride
envy
slander
 so that I'm screwed
 at first glance
but went ahead and looked the words up
in the strict no-nonsense OED
and compared other Bible translations
especially for sensuality
that one sticky and worrying.

Sensuality—lewdness—lewdness
Lewdness—having a desire for sex sins—
Lustful desires

A gratification of the senses; self-indulgence
[sexually or in regard to food and drink]
voluptuous
as in tending to or occupied with sensual pleasure
licentious
as in immoral, especially in sexual relations
disregarding accepted rules or conventions
hedonism—out of balance—idol
lascivious = lustful [sensuality]

Oh okay
so then it's not the thing where
you swoon at the whisky-and-clove aroma
of Lucky Tiger hair tonic
or roll your naked self up in a big wad of velvet
when no one's at home
or look ever so forward to

every last aspect of the afternoon cig

rather
more of a willful rebellious
middle-finger-at-God type of gullet-cramming
and whoring around
and the thing one forgets is
how the Law was put there
to throw into stark relief
our inability to keep it.

And that should be a kind of comfort you know.

[#5]

After hoarding CD #5
in the 6-CD Hollies box set
[Clarke-Hicks-Nash Years]
it suddenly seemed the time
to trot it out
to accompany the baking of an oblong butter cake
mortared and enrobed with Hershey's frosting
for the Bible-study gals [Hide the Cramps records!!]

Two of the [Hollies] songs I knew
from a Greatest Hits tape I'd bought in 1988
had hardly heard them since
and that revival was weird!
just weird!
Flashes of old pale-blue bedroom
cat on the bed
loving their accents
overcome with drum-lust
and probably
pining for some blonde-haired
earring'd Pizza Boy
or dark underprivileged
high-school baseball-player.

[𝄢]

We were speaking of bass players
Tall-calm-stolid
And in old days
you couldn't have a beat group without one.
Just picture the Beatles
their 3 guitarists drawing straws to choose a bass player
John: not it! Geo: not it! Paul: hell yeah!
But never mind them.

Eric Haydock all rugged & Mancunian
but otherwise the spitting image of my
Republican brother-in-law
a welcome addition to our frenzied family
as he is so *mellow*.
Bless him. Not the beat-group type at all
[once when all the others had obligations I joked 'Well, Brian, let's us go have a beer, then!' but the remark seemed to confound him].
But that's just as well—
Haydock wasn't the beat-group type either in the end
Though on bass he *killed* it.
He left shrugging in a whirlwind of mental-breakdown rumors...

Then Bernie swooped in to fill the hole
and one stalks the suitable tribute
but is full of brandy and the hour is ridiculous
Mr. Quiet & Anonymous & Very Nice in Turtlenecks
hiding face behind hands & wedding ring
Weighty eyelids defying scrutiny
imparting kind of a sweet stoned look
the wedge between lower lashes and nose
fitted to the lips of a lover
estranged by time and space.

[Too Personal or Unguarded or Something]

"I don't sneeze in public"
said the guy at the library
and heck that's
funny
I'd thought myself all alone
in that neurosis.
Seriously.
I can't do it if anyone's looking.

[Cheers, Jerky]

Hello ludicrous character in the bathroom mirror
do you know what I want?
do you know what I want?
To delight him
even when I fail at housework
which is often
and lately, always.
Hai ziveli absurd figure reflected in the toaster.
You know what your problem is.
All too frequent your arguments with Our Lord
All too habitual your bosh-and-flimshaw at spouse
Far too pen-prone, you.
Pride/foolishness/Hey there Ridiculous.
If I hadn't been a freak so long
If I hadn't been a freak so long
Why did God let me be a freak for so long?
Why did my mother tell me that was all right?
Prost, mutant.
Noroc.
You freak.

[Front Manic]

Allan Clarke [Hollies]
and
Jim Morrison [Doors]
are not what you'd call
twin types
but they do me just the same
almost.
Don't look for too long
 or start to burn up inside
but go on listen
listen for days.

[Upsides: History, Tech, & Passionate Crackpot]

Dreary February
and too many old Hollies films
viewed with girl-eyes
thinking
[of guitarist]
'personal chemistry
and laws of symmetry
and cultural beauty standards
dictate:
that one is a knockout'
and if viewing attracts notice at home
only claim to be studying guitar techniques
[always encouraged]
But then
guitarist-eyes skated in unseen
and learning took place unawares
Such as F [and D]
and C minor
formed all down fretboard
result in *every possible chord!*
[minus fancy ones]
Plus professional affirmation of novice habit:
adding pinky finger to vary chords & add interest
How [and why] to strum less angrily
or more frantically
as situation warrants
and
and
[quite by accident; it was acquired during our Jam phase]
we have almost the very same
Rickenbacker.

[The English Beat-Group School of Shitty Mothering]

In January
        timid steps out of
        my murky cocoon of woe
        and into the daily

leaning heavily on English beat groups
in black-white-grey
and the splendor of their drainpipe trousers
their glowing accented words
calculated to woo.
Their guitars my church bells.

Today:
Lunch:
mundane cheese sandwich
coffee and
cigarettes
and bitter epiphanies
of a summer vacation squandered
discipline? little
frivolous fun? not much of it
100°? Emotional storms? Stubborn &
shrewish bitchery? Guitar fondling?
Preoccupation with foreign musicians older than my father?

Nearly every day.
All of it.

Mothering.
I was once so *LOFTY* about it.
So lofty so smug so capable
so stung by life's blows

and now throwing it all away
heaven's good gifts

for guitar prowess
mostly imagined.

[Life & Style]

"Yeah"—he nodded as I lit a cigarette
to accompany peach brandy
on the back porch
"I'll be burying your ass"
[we sometimes ruminate over which of us will die first]
and I could only agree with him.
I'm always thinking: Of course he'll bury my ass.
Only one in four of my grandparents
lived past the age of 65
the others all snarled up in cancer & liquor & diabetes & bum tickers
two of them never seeing 50
besides which
my tendency to get all wound up
and then broody & crushed & persecuted
which does the health no good at all they say.

And yet

that one hardy forefather
did smoke and drink
a fair bit in his day
lived to 85
lived somewhat as I do
smoke & drink & garden
& messing around
on stringed instruments
& sitting for hours
out back in the shade

Besides
in looks I favor him
[the Polish side of the family]
so a lucky break
on the longevity score

surely isn't out of the question
and that type of optimistic thinking
does all kinds of mystical healing jazz

probably.

www.ingramcontent.com/pod-product-compliance
Lightning Source LLC
Chambersburg PA
CBHW060812050426
42449CB00008B/1642